Contents

Shalom!

My name is Margaret Jacobi, and I am a rabbi. A rabbi is a Jewish teacher and leader. Both men and women can be rabbis.

All over the world, Jews meet and pray to God at places called synagogues. I am the rabbi at Birmingham Progressive Synagogue.

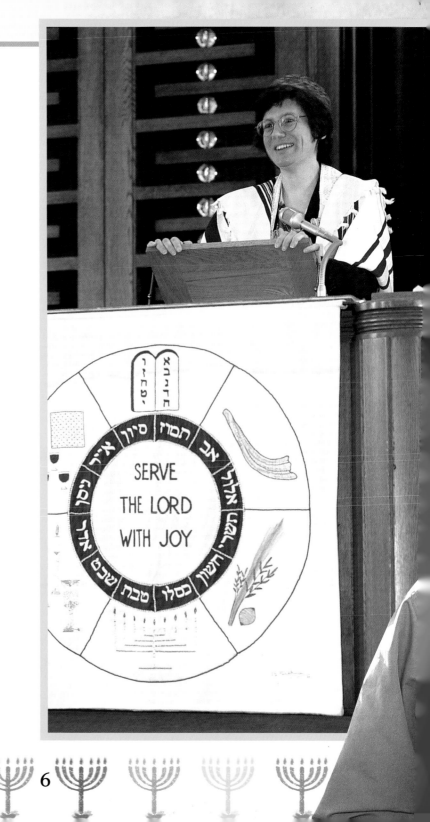

My father is a rabbi too, so when I was growing up I saw the work that he did. Later I went to college to train to be a rabbi.

Today I live with my husband David and our son Yoni.

Becoming a rabbi

I trained for five years to become a rabbi.
I had to study the Bible, the Hebrew language
and the history of the Jewish people.

Hebrew was the language
that the first Jews spoke,
long ago in the Middle East.
Today, Jews everywhere still
say prayers in Hebrew.

There is some Hebrew writing
underneath the word Rabbi
on my coffee mug. It says
'Shalom, rabbi!'

I also learned how to lead Jewish services and ceremonies, such as blessing a new baby.

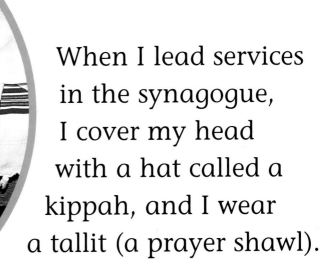

When I lead services in the synagogue, I cover my head with a hat called a kippah, and I wear a tallit (a prayer shawl).

The Torah

The first part of the Jewish Bible is called the Torah. It tells us about the first Jews and the Ten Commandments and other laws that God gave them.

The Torah is written in Hebrew on special scrolls. We keep the scrolls in a cupboard called the Ark, at the front of the synagogue.

The velvet covers on the scrolls are embroidered with Jewish symbols, such as the six-pointed star and the menorah (a candlestick with seven branches).

When we read from a scroll, we use a silver pointer called a yad to keep our place.

Shabbat

Shabbat is the Hebrew name for the seventh day of the week. It lasts from sunset on Friday to sunset on Saturday.

One of the Ten Commandments tells us to keep Shabbat holy, and so we make it different from all the other days of the week.

On Friday evenings we light candles at home to welcome Shabbat. There is also a short service at the synagogue.

On Saturday mornings we have a longer service at the synagogue. I take a Torah scroll from the Ark and sometimes the children 'undress' it. Then we open the scroll, ready to read.

First I read aloud from the Torah scroll in
Hebrew. Then I repeat the reading in English,
so that everyone at the service can understand.

We read a different part of the Torah each
Shabbat so that, in one year, we go from the
beginning to the end. Then we start again!

After the reading we lift the scroll high so that everyone in the synagogue can see it.

During the service the children come for a special blessing under my tallit.

Kiddush

After the service I say a blessing called Kiddush before we drink a little wine. Then we eat plaited bread called challah. The children hand round the bread for everyone at the synagogue to share.

Ending Shabbat

Saturday afternoon is a peaceful time at home.

At sunset, we mark the end of Shabbat with prayers called Havdalah. We light a plaited candle and we smell a special jar of sweet spices as we pray for a sweet week ahead.

Learning

On Sunday mornings the children and young people come to our religion school at the synagogue. They learn about being Jewish.

I teach the oldest class. We read Jewish prayers and stories, and we talk about growing up and what it means to be a Jew.

The youngest class hear stories from the Bible and make pictures about them.

All the classes and teachers join together for an assembly, where we sing songs and tell Jewish stories.

Special days

When Jewish boys are 13, they can become Bar Mitzvah, and when girls are 12 or 13, they can become Bat Mitzvah. It means that the boy or girl is beginning to be a grown-up.

I help the young people to study, to get ready for their Bar or Bat Mitzvah day at our synagogue.

On this special day the Bar Mitzvah boy or Bat Mitzvah girl reads in Hebrew from the Torah scroll. Then there is a party for all the family.

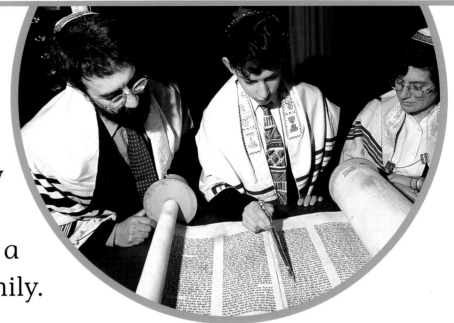

A wedding is another very special day. The couple stand with me under the chuppah, or canopy, while I read the wedding service.

Festivals

I love celebrating the Jewish festivals each year.

Rosh Hashanah, the Jewish New Year, comes in the autumn. We welcome the new year by blowing the shofar, a ram's horn.

Then we eat apples dipped in honey, as we pray for a sweet new year.

22

In winter we celebrate Chanukah. For eight evenings we light candles – and we give presents to the children, too.

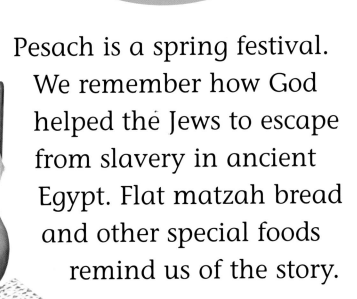

Pesach is a spring festival. We remember how God helped the Jews to escape from slavery in ancient Egypt. Flat matzah bread and other special foods remind us of the story.

Working life

It's a busy life being a rabbi! There is always lots of office work to be done with Rosa, the synagogue administrator.

I use my computer to write sermons or lessons, and to keep in touch with Jewish communities around the world.

We are building a new synagogue here. I have to check the building plans with our chairman, who helps to run the synagogue.

Our community

Our synagogue is a friendly place, where many people come to meet and learn. We have a lunchtime club for members of the synagogue to talk and share ideas.

It's important for me to care for all the members of the synagogue. I visit those who are old or sick.

I often meet the vicar of the local church to discuss the needs of our neighbourhood. We also work with the monks at the Buddhist pagoda nearby. It is good to learn about each other's religions.

Glossary

Note: Many Hebrew words contain the sound 'ch', as in the Scottish word 'loch'.

Bar Mitzvah/Bat Mitzvah
Hebrew for 'Son of the Commandment'/'Daughter of the Commandment'. Becoming Bar or Bat Mitzvah means starting to be a Jewish grown-up.

Bible
The Jews' holy book. The Jewish or Hebrew Bible is almost the same as the Christian Old Testament.

blessing
A type of prayer to God.

challah
Soft white bread, often in a plaited shape, baked for Shabbat.

Chanukah
A Jewish festival which remembers how, 2,000 years ago, Jews won back their temple in Jerusalem from their enemies.

chuppah
A special canopy under which Jewish weddings take place. It is a reminder of a Jewish home.

Commandments
Laws from God guiding the Jewish people on how to live. The Ten Commandments are the main laws.

community

A group of people who live close together or share beliefs or interests.

holy

To do with God.

matzah

Flat bread – a reminder of the Jews who escaped from Egypt. They had no time to let their bread rise before they baked it, so it turned out flat.

Pesach

A Jewish festival which remembers the Jews' escape from slavery. The English name for Pesach is Passover.

pray/prayer

To pray means to think about or talk to God. A prayer is the words you think or say when you pray.

Progressive

One branch of the Jewish religion, which gives women an equal role.

sermon

A special talk during a service.

service

A meeting in the synagogue to pray to God.

Shabbat

A special day of rest each week, when Jews go to synagogue and spend time with their families.

Shalom

A Hebrew greeting. It can mean 'Hello', 'Goodbye' and 'Peace'.

synagogue

A place where Jewish people go to meet, pray and learn.

Index